WHEN I LOVED MYSELF ENOUGH

KIM McMILLEN

with Alison McMillen

St. Martin's Press ✖ New York

To contact the author: alimcmillen@yahoo.com

www.stmartins.com

Design by Michael Collica

ISBN: 0-312-27124-7

10 9 8 7 6 5 4

TO MY ALi GIRL

AN EXTRAORDINARY DAUGHTER
WHO ALWAYS KNEW I WASN'T
BORN YESTERDAY.

INTRODUCTION

FOR MANY YEARS I LIVED WITH
A GUARDED HEART. I DID NOT
KNOW HOW TO EXTEND LOVE AND
COMPASSION TO MYSELF. IN MY
40th YEAR THAT BEGAN CHANGING.

AS I GREW TO LOVE ALL OF WHO I AM
LIFE STARTED CHANGING IN BEAUTIFUL
AND MYSTERIOUS WAYS. MY HEART
SOFTENED AND I BEGAN TO SEE
THROUGH VERY DIFFERENT EYES.

MY COMMITMENT TO FOLLOW THIS CALL-ING GREW STRONG AND IN THE PROCESS A DIVINE INTELLIGENCE CAME TO GUIDE MY LIFE. I BELIEVE THIS EVER PRESENT RESOURCE IS GRACE AND IS AVAILABLE TO US ALL.

FOR THE PAST 12 YEARS I HAVE BEEN LEARNING TO RECOGNIZE AND ACCEPT THIS GIFT. CULTIVATING LOVE AND COMPASSION FOR MYSELF MADE IT POSSIBLE.

THE FOLLOWING STEPS ARE UNIQUELY MINE. YOURS WILL LOOK DIFFERENT. BUT I DO HOPE MINE GIVE VOICE TO A HUNGER YOU MAY SHARE.

WHEN I LOVED MYSELF ENOUGH

I QUIT SETTLING FOR TOO LITTLE.

WHEN I LOVED MYSELF ENOUGH

I CAME TO KNOW MY OWN
GOODNESS

WHEN I LOVED MYSELF ENOUGH

I BEGAN TAKING THE GIFT OF
LIFE SERIOUSLY AND GRATEFULLY.

WHEN I LOVED MYSELF ENOUGH

I BEGAN TO KNOW I WAS IN THE
RIGHT PLACE AT THE RIGHT TIME

AND I COULD RELAX.

WHEN I LOVED MYSELF ENOUGH

I FELT COMPELLED TO SLOW DOWN
WAY DOWN

AND THAT HAS MADE ALL
THE DIFFERENCE.

WHEN I LOVED MYSELF ENOUGH

I BOUGHT A FEATHER BED.

6

WHEN I LOVED MYSELF ENOUGH

I CAME TO LOVE BEING ALONE
SURROUNDED BY SILENCE
AWED BY ITS SPELL
LISTENING TO INNER SPACE

WHEN I LOVED MYSELF ENOUGH

I CAME TO SEE I AM NOT
SPECIAL
BUT I AM UNIQUE.

WHEN I LOVED MYSELF ENOUGH

I REDEFINED SUCCESS AND LIFE
BECAME SIMPLE. OH, THE
PLEASURE IN THAT.

WHEN I LOVED MYSELF ENOUGH

I CAME TO KNOW I AM WORTHY
OF KNOWING GOD DIRECTLY.

WHEN I LOVED MYSELF ENOUGH

I BEGAN TO SEE I DIDN'T HAVE TO
CHASE AFTER LIFE. IF I AM
QUIET AND HOLD STILL, LIFE
COMES TO ME.

WHEN I LOVED MYSELF ENOUGH

I GAVE UP THE BELIEF THAT
LIFE IS HARD.

WHEN I LOVED MYSELF ENOUGH

I CAME TO SEE EMOTIONAL PAIN
IS A SIGNAL I AM OPERATING
OUTSIDE TRUTH.

WHEN I LOVED MYSELF ENOUGH

I LET THE TOMBOY IN ME
SWING OFF THE ROPE IN JACKASS
CANYON.   YES!

WHEN I LOVED MYSELF ENOUGH

I LEARNED TO MEET MY OWN
NEEDS AND NOT CALL IT SELFISH.

WHEN I LOVED MYSELF ENOUGH

THE PARTS OF ME LONG IGNORED,
THE ORPHANS OF MY SOUL, QUIT
VYING FOR ATTENTION. THAT
WAS THE BEGINNING OF INNER
PEACE. THEN I BEGAN SEEING
CLEARLY.

WHEN I LOVED MYSELF ENOUGH

I BEGAN TO SEE THAT DESIRES
OF THE HEART DO COME, AND
I GREW MORE PATIENT AND CALM,
EXCEPT WHEN I FORGET.

WHEN I LOVED MYSELF ENOUGH

I QUIT IGNORING OR TOLERATING
MY PAIN.

WHEN I LOVED MYSELF ENOUGH

I STARTED FEELING ALL MY FEELINGS,
NOT ANALYZING THEM — REALLY FEELING
THEM.
WHEN I DO, SOMETHING AMAZING
HAPPENS. TRY IT. YOU WILL SEE.

WHEN I LOVED MYSELF ENOUGH

MY HEART BECAME SO TENDER
IT COULD WELCOME JOY AND
SORROW EQUALLY.

WHEN I LOVED MYSELF ENOUGH

I STARTED MEDITATING EVERYDAY.
THIS IS A PROFOUND ACT OF
SELF LOVE.

WHEN I LOVED MYSELF ENOUGH

I CAME TO ~~FEEL~~ LIKE A GIFT TO
THE WORLD AND I COLLECTED
BEAUTIFUL RIBBONS AND BOWS.
THEY STILL HANG ON MY WALL
TO REMIND ME.

WHEN I LOVED MYSELF ENOUGH

I LEARNED TO ASK, "WHO IN ME IS FEELING THIS WAY" WHEN I FEEL ANXIOUS, ANGRY, RESTLESS OR SAD.

IF I LISTEN PATIENTLY I DISCOVER WHO NEEDS MY LOVE.

23

WHEN I LOVED MYSELF ENOUGH

I NO LONGER NEEDED THINGS OR
PEOPLE TO MAKE ME FEEL SAFE.

WHEN I LOVED MYSELF ENOUGH

I QUIT WISHING MY LIFE LOOKED
SOME OTHER WAY AND BEGAN TO
SEE THAT AS IT IS, MY LIFE SERVES
MY EVOLUTION.

WHEN I LOVED MYSELF ENOUGH

I BEGAN TO COMPREHEND THE
COMPLEXITY, MYSTERY AND VASTNESS
OF MY SOUL. HOW FOOLISH TO
THINK I CAN KNOW THE MEANING
OF ANOTHER'S LIFE

WHEN I LOVED MYSELF ENOUGH

I QUIT PROJECTING MY STRENGTHS
AND WEAKNESSES ON TO OTHERS
AND KEPT THEM AS MY OWN.

WHEN I LOVED MYSELF ENOUGH

I BEGAN TO FEEL A DIVINE
PRESENCE IN ME AND HEAR
ITS GUIDANCE.

I AM LEARNING TO TRUST THIS
AND LIVE FROM IT.

WHEN I LOVED MYSELF ENOUGH

I QUIT EXHAUSTING MYSELF
BY TRYING SO HARD.

WHEN I LOVED MYSELF ENOUGH

I BEGAN FEELING A COMMUNITY
WITHIN. THIS INNER TEAM WITH
DIVERSE TALENTS AND IDIOSYNCRACIES
IS MY STRENGTH AND MY POTENTIAL

WE HOLD TEAM MEETINGS.

WHEN I LOVED MYSELF ENOUGH

I STOPPED BLAMING MYSELF FOR
CHOICES I HAD MADE — WHICH
MADE ME FEEL SAFE AND I TOOK
RESPONSIBILITY FOR THEM.

WHEN I LOVED MYSELF ENOUGH

I BEGAN SEEING THE ABUSE
IN TRYING TO FORCE SOMETHING
OR SOMEONE WHO ISN'T READY —
INCLUDING ME.

WHEN I LOVED MYSELF ENOUGH

I BEGAN WALKING AND TAKING
THE STAIRS EVERY CHANCE I GET,
AND CHOOSING THE SCENIC
ROUTE.

WHEN I LOVED MYSELF ENOUGH

I BECAME MY OWN AUTHORITY
BY LISTENING TO THE WISDOM OF
MY HEART. THIS IS HOW GOD
SPEAKS TO ME. THIS IS INTUITION.

WHEN I LOVED MYSELF ENOUGH

I BEGAN FEELING SUCH RELIEF.

WHEN I LOVED MYSELF ENOUGH

THE IMPULSIVE PART OF ME
LEARNED TO WAIT FOR THE
RIGHT TIME. THEN I BECOME
CLEAR AND UNAFRAID.

WHEN I LOVED MYSELF ENOUGH

I BEGAN TO ACCEPT THE
UNACCEPTABLE.

WHEN I LOVED MYSELF ENOUGH

I BEGAN TO SEE THAT MY EGO IS
PART OF MY SOUL. WITH THIS
SHIFT IN PERCEPTION IT LOST
ITS STRIDENCY AND PARANOIA,
AND COULD DO ITS JOB.

WHEN I LOVED MYSELF ENOUGH

I WOULD SOMETIMES WAKE IN THE
NIGHT TO MUSIC PLAYING WITHIN
ME.

WHEN I LOVED MYSELF ENOUGH

I BEGAN LEAVING WHATEVER WASN'T
HEALTHY. THIS MEANT PEOPLE, JOBS,
MY OWN BELIEFS AND HABITS —
ANYTHING THAT KEPT ME SMALL.
MY JUDGMENT CALLED IT DISLOYAL.
NOW I SEE IT AS SELF LOVING.

40

WHEN I LOVED MYSELF ENOUGH

I GAVE UP PERFECTIONISM —
THAT KILLER OF JOY.

WHEN I LOVED MYSELF ENOUGH

I COULD TELL THE TRUTH ABOUT
MY GIFTS AND MY LIMITATIONS.

WHEN I LOVED MYSELF ENOUGH

I QUIT ANSWERING THE TELEPHONE
WHEN I DON'T WANT TO TALK.

WHEN I LOVED MYSELF ENOUGH

FORGIVING OTHERS BECAME
IRRELEVANT.

WHEN I LOVED MYSELF ENOUGH

I COULD REMEMBER, DURING
TIMES OF CONFUSION, STRUGGLE OR
GRIEF, THAT THESE TOO ARE
PART OF ME AND DESERVE MY
LOVE.

WHEN I LOVED MYSELF ENOUGH

I COULD ALLOW MY HEART TO
BURST WIDE OPEN AND TAKE
IN THE PAIN OF THE WORLD.

WHEN I LOVED MYSELF ENOUGH

I STARTED PICKING UP LITTER
ON THE STREET.

47

WHEN I LOVED MYSELF ENOUGH

I COULD FEEL GOD IN ME AND
SEE GOD IN YOU. THAT MAKES
US DIVINE !
ARE YOU READY FOR THAT ?

WHEN I LOVED MYSELF ENOUGH

I STARTED WRITING ABOUT MY
LIFE AND VIEWS BECAUSE I
KNEW THIS WAS MY RIGHT AND
MY RESPONSIBILITY.

WHEN I LOVED MYSELF ENOUGH

I BEGAN TO SEE MY PURPOSE
AND GENTLY WEAN MYSELF FROM
DISTRACTIONS.

WHEN I LOVED MYSELF ENOUGH

I SAW THAT WHAT I RESISTED PERSISTED,
LIKE A SMALL CHILD TUGGING MY
SKIRT. NOW I AM CURIOUS AND
GENTLE WHEN RESISTANCE COMES
TUGGING.

WHEN I LOVED MYSELF ENOUGH

I LEARNED TO STOP WHAT I AM
DOING, IF EVEN FOR A MOMENT,
AND COMFORT THE PART OF ME
WHO IS SCARED.

WHEN I LOVED MYSELF ENOUGH

I LEARNED TO SAY NO WHEN I
WANT TO AND YES WHEN I WANT
TO.

WHEN I LOVED MYSELF ENOUGH

I SAW BEYOND RIGHT AND WRONG
AND BECAME NEUTRAL. AT FIRST
I THOUGHT THIS WAS INDIFFERENCE;

NOW I SEE THE CLARITY THAT
COMES WITH NEUTRALITY.

WHEN I LOVED MYSELF ENOUGH

I BEGAN TO FEED MY HUNGER FOR
SOLITUDE AND REVEL IN THE
INEXPLICABLE CONTENTMENT THAT
IS ITS COMPANION.

WHEN I LOVED MYSELF ENOUGH

I COULD SEE HOW FUNNY LIFE IS,
HOW FUNNY I AM
AND HOW FUNNY YOU ARE.

WHEN I LOVED MYSELF ENOUGH

I RECOGNIZED MY COURAGE AND
FEAR, MY NAIVETE AND WISDOM,
AND I MAKE A PLACE FOR EACH
AT MY TABLE.

WHEN I LOVED MYSELF ENOUGH

I STARTED TREATING MYSELF TO A
MASSAGE AT LEAST ONCE A MONTH.

WHEN I LOVED MYSELF ENOUGH

I REALIZED I AM NEVER ALONE.

WHEN I LOVED MYSELF ENOUGH

I STOPPED FEARING EMPTY TIME
AND QUIT MAKING PLANS. NOW
I DO WHAT FEELS RIGHT AND AM
IN STEP WITH MY OWN RHYTHMS.

DELICIOUS !

WHEN I LOVED MYSELF ENOUGH

I QUIT TRYING TO IMPRESS
MY BROTHER.

WHEN I LOVED MYSELF ENOUGH

I STOPPED TRYING TO BANISH THE
CRITICAL VOICES FROM MY HEAD.
NOW I SAY " THANK YOU FOR
YOUR VIEWS " AND THEY FEEL
HEARD.   END OF DISCUSSION.

62

WHEN I LOVED MYSELF ENOUGH

I LET THE PART OF ME THAT STILL
MISSES KENT FEEL SAD INSTEAD
OF TRYING TO STOP HER FROM
LOVING HIM.

WHEN I LOVED MYSELF ENOUGH

I BEGAN BUYING A HOSTESS FRUIT
PIE FOR THE TEENAGER IN ME WHO
LOVES THEM SO.   ONCE IN AWHILE.

CHERRY.

WHEN I LOVED MYSELF ENOUGH

I QUIT TRYING TO BE A SAVIOR
FOR OTHERS.

WHEN I LOVED MYSELF ENOUGH

I LOST MY FEAR OF SPEAKING
MY TRUTH FOR I HAVE COME
TO SEE HOW GOOD IT IS.

WHEN I LOVED MYSELF ENOUGH

I BEGAN POURING MY FEELINGS
INTO MY JOURNALS. THESE LOVING
COMPANIONS SPEAK MY LANGUAGE.
NO TRANSLATION NEEDED.

WHEN I LOVED MYSELF ENOUGH

I STOPPED SEEKING "EXPERTS" AND
STARTED LIVING MY LIFE.

WHEN I LOVED MYSELF ENOUGH

I CAME TO SEE HOW MY ANGER
TEACHES ABOUT RESPONSIBILITY
AND MY ARROGANCE TEACHES
ABOUT HUMILITY, SO I LISTEN
TO BOTH CAREFULLY.

WHEN I LOVED MYSELF ENOUGH

I STARTED EATING ORGANICALLY
GROWN FOOD (EXCEPT FOR
THOSE OCCASIONAL FRUIT PIES
OF COURSE).

WHEN I LOVED MYSELF ENOUGH

I COULD BE AT EASE WITH THE
COMINGS AND GOINGS OF
JUDGMENT AND DESPAIR

WHEN I LOVED MYSELF ENOUGH

I WAS ABLE TO BE TREATED TO
A $50 HAIRCUT AND ENJOY
EVERY MINUTE OF IT.

WHEN I LOVED MYSELF ENOUGH

I QUIT HAVING TO BE RIGHT
WHICH MAKES BEING WRONG
MEANINGLESS.

73

WHEN I LOVED MYSELF ENOUGH

I LEARNED TO GRIEVE THE HURTS
IN LIFE WHEN THEY HAPPEN INSTEAD
OF MAKING MY HEART HEAVY
FROM LUGGING THEM AROUND.

WHEN I LOVED MYSELF ENOUGH

I FORGAVE MYSELF FOR ALL
THE TIMES I THOUGHT I WASN'T
GOOD ENOUGH.

WHEN I LOVED MYSELF ENOUGH

THINGS GOT REAL QUIET INSIDE.
NICE. REAL NICE.

WHEN I LOVED MYSELF ENOUGH

I BEGAN LISTENING TO THE WISDOM
OF MY BODY. IT SPEAKS SO
CLEARLY THROUGH ITS FATIGUE,
SENSITIVITIES, AVERSIONS AND
HUNGERS.

WHEN I LOVED MYSELF ENOUGH

I QUIT FEARING MY FEAR.

WHEN I LOVED MYSELF ENOUGH

I QUIT REHASHING THE PAST AND
WORRYING ABOUT THE FUTURE WHICH
KEEPS ME IN THE PRESENT WHERE
ALIVENESS LIVES.

WHEN I LOVED MYSELF ENOUGH

I REALIZED MY MIND CAN TORMENT
AND DECEIVE ME, BUT IN THE
SERVICE OF MY HEART IT IS A
GREAT AND NOBLE ALLY.

WHEN I LOVED MYSELF ENOUGH

I BEGAN TO TASTE FREEDOM.

WHEN I LOVED MYSELF ENOUGH

I FOUND MY VOICE AND WROTE
THIS LITTLE BOOK.

About the Author

My mother died in September of 1996, at the age of 52, only a few short months after writing this book. She was not ill and did not know that she was going to die. Her death was very sudden and it deeply shocked everyone who knew her. It has been very difficult for me, as well as her friends and family, to cope with life without her. She died too young, and I am aware of her absence every waking moment

One thing that has made grieving for her more tolerable has been this book. Following her lead, I continued to publish it out of my home. It has been extremely rewarding work. I have received countless letters and phone calls from people all over the world who have been touched by the wisdom of my moms words. They tell me that they feel as though, through the book, they have come to know Kim McMillen. I could not agree more.

This book is my mother. Its message is what she spent years meditating on, reading and writing about, and experiencing. It is everything she believed in, and everything she brought me up to believe in. It is her autobiography, her declaration, her <u>soul</u>.

Even though she didnt know she was nearing the end of her life, she knew on some level that she had to express the things that she had learned to be true. After many years filled with self doubt and self criticism, she decided to devote herself to finding self compassion. When she did, and was able to write her findings down for others to read, her life was complete, and sadly came to an end.

I have a constant ache in my heart, a longing to see her again in this world. She was an amazing mother, friend, writer, business consultant, chaplain, river runner, dog lover, neighbor, and woman. Although I miss her terribly, I am comforted by the knowledge that, as this book is the truest expression of who my mom was, in its continued existence, what she had to offer to the world will live on.

Alison Ucmillen, January 2001

Acknowledgements

I wish to express my deepest thanks to all the people who helped to keep the book alive for the past four years:

My dad, Todd McMillen, Jeffy Griffin's John Davis, Myrta Velez, John Boyer, Jill Jones, Penny Triggs, Win's Cynda Johnson and many others who have helped the books creation and distribution, not to mention my sanity.

In addition, many many thanks to Jennifer Enderlin, who had the vision to take the book into the big leagues.

Thank you all, this could not have happened with out you!